To Jan with love from [signature]

The Book
of
Now

by Leah Shelleda

After the Jug Was Broken

The Book of Now

Poetry for the Rising Tide

edited by

Leah Shelleda

The Book of Now
Copyright © 2012 by Fisher King Press
All rights reserved.
First Edition
ISBN 978-1-926715-90-2

Published simultaneously in Canada and the United States of America by Fisher King Press. For information on obtaining permission for use of material from this work, submit a written request to:

permissions@fisherkingpress.com

Fisher King Press
PO Box 222321
Carmel, CA 93922
www.fisherkingpress.com
fisherking@fisherkingpress.com
+1-831-238-7799

"The War Works Hard," "The Prisoner," "Bag of Bones," "I Was In a Hurry," "Shoemaker," "The Jewel," and "Travel Agency" by Dunya Mikhail, translated by Elizabeth Winslow, from THE WAR WORKS HARD, copyright ©2005 by Dunya Mikhail. Reprinted by permission of New Directions Publishing Corp.

ACKNOWLEDGMENTS

I want to express my gratitude to my husband Bill Fulton, partner and cover artist. I am so grateful to the poets whose work appears in this book for their generosity and help. Thanks to my publishers Mel Mathews and Patty Cabanas, and to my friends and family who support and nourish me.

Many thanks to all who have provided permission to quote their works. Some of the poems in this collection have been published in the following literary magazines or books - sometimes in an earlier version.

Jane Downs: "The Weight of Pink Peonies" first appeared in *Rhino, The Poetry Forum*, 2009; "To Katherine" *Marin Poetry Center Anthology*, 2004, "Spring" & "The Minotaur," *Psychological Perspectives*, Volume 51, Issue 1, 2008.

Anita Endrezze: "Calendars," "Calypso," and "Song Maker" from *at the helm of twilight*, Broken Moon Press, Seattle, WA, 1992. "Song of our Times" from *Breaking Edges*, Red Bird Chapbooks, Pepin, Wisconsin 2012, with permission of the author.

Crystal Good: "Boom Boom," "passing wrong," "in new england," "vw mourning," from *Valley Girl*, www.crystalgood.net, with permission of the author.

Frances Hatfield: "Rough Guide to the Underworld," Jung Journal: Culture and Psyche, Vol. 6, No. 3 (Summer 2012), published by the San Francisco Jung Institute and University of California Press, "Just Like A Woman," first published in the Anthology of Monterey Bay Poets, Chatoyant Press, 2004, "Monday Night Cancer Group," "The Talking Cure," "The Soul's Geometry," from *Rudiments of Flight*, Wing Press, San Antonio, Texas, to be published Fall 2012. With permission of the author.

Naomi Ruth Lowinsky: "Where Coyote Bush Roams," *Fourth River*.

Dunya Mikhail: "The War Works Hard," "The Prisoner," "Bag of Bones," "I Was In a Hurry," "Shoemaker," "The Jewel," and "Travel Agency" by Dunya Mikhail, translated by Elizabeth Winslow, from THE WAR WORKS HARD, copyright ©2005 by Dunya Mikhail. Reprinted by permission of New Directions Publishing Corp.

Leah Shelleda: "Extinct Birds," first published by Jung Journal, Culture and Psyche, Volume 3, Number 4, Fall 2009. Published by Jung Institute of San Francisco, and University of California Press, "The End of Abundance," *After the Jug Was Broken*, with permission of Fisher King Press.

CONTENTS

For Bill
All grandchildren, born into climate change
and
White Shell Woman

INTRODUCTION

I always begin with questions, but I was not even sure what the question was when I began working on this book. Was the question "What Do We Need to Hear From Poetry?" or "What Is Poetry Saying?"

I decided on the latter. What I had to do, I told myself, was listen to the voices, and listen for those who understand the present, and know the future will not be the same. (Do you too feel the ground shaking sometimes, or do you live somewhere other than the edge of a shifting continent?)

I did have other questions: Was there a shift in consciousness? Not that I would turn away from a sparkling alternative, or a vision with the word 'hope' in it. Only please, no Certainty. We are sometimes overwhelmed by those who are Certain - of Apocalypse, Mayan or Christian, of Redemption, or a Brave New World.

The poets in this book understand that they should at least try to hold the opposites, as Rilke did. They do not deny for a moment that there is terror in the world, but they still recognize beauty and they often find it in the wild, though beauty shows up in the damnedest places.

The Deconstruction pandemic seems to be over. It is now safe to say, as these poets do, that meaning matters, even if there are no Ultimate Meanings. I wanted to include poets who pierced me, who took my breath away. That wasn't a challenge, a gauntlet thrown down - simply how we can respond to poetry. (Besides, I've exchanged my academic gauntlets for gardening gloves).

And these poets can write. Language is everyone's tool, but these poets truly enjoy playing with language, and it's a game they

1

are good at. No, I *don't* mean that poetry is a game, only that the play of language is pleasurable.

And these poets are musical - ranging from single notes to symphony and chant. They are not afraid of rhythm, despite the fact that poetry has been dancing away from it as though all poetic music was the feared iambic pentameter. These are imaginative poets, but their words alone can have their way with me. I have a bias that these poets share: We believe that all life has value, and we wish to preserve it. One of us has lived through war, knows it intimately, and writes about it as a universal fire that flares up in many parts of the globe.

And some of us write of the Old Ways, because we feel that something vital, something earth-enlivening, has been lost. Our poems can be calendars marking feasts, and sacrifice and ceremonies long forgotten. And some of us have visited the places known as the Underworld and the DreamRealm, and when the terror subsides we find remnants of the journey, and some call that wisdom, and others call it essential if we are going to make into the next century.

Who doesn't fear a future our countries are unable to prepare for? We don't know the length of a bridge, the height of the seas, or the size of an ark. How wonderful it would be if poetry, these poets, could be a bridge. Or perhaps a nest - not in the sense of comfort and cozy, but as the place where something cracks open and something new emerges. Something that can fly. Ezra Pound said that poetry should build a world.

And if, in my desires for this book, I fly too close to the sun, I'll join you on this beautiful earth - reading aloud to each other as time comes toward us.

ANITA ENDREZZE

"Even grass has a song,'though only wind hears it."

When I first found Anita Endrezze's poems, I felt I had come home. Here was the passion, the eloquence, the originality, the insistent song, that I longed to find. But how could I feel so at home? Endrezze is half-West European, half-Yaqui, her origins, her culture so far from mine.

I have lamented the loss of the indigenous cultures of the world, languages no longer spoken, material culture no longer used, but consigned to museums or for sale in the marketplace, their home on earth desacrilized. We of the Privileged World careen down a path with terrible consequences, and what alternatives, what native knowledge have we lost? Now, we may only meet native people in a space of neglect and need, their pride and identity demeaned.

In *Song Maker*, Endrezze writes about a "drunk on Main Avenue, slumped in front of the Union Gospel Mission." We might try to avoid looking at him as we pass, might feel empathy or fight off disgust, but Endrezze knows who he was, hears his voice:

> Didn't he make songs people still sing
> in their sleep?
> Didn't coyotes beg him for new songs

3

to give to the moon?
Didn't he dance all night once and laugh
when the women suddenly turned
shy at dawn

By the end of the poem, she has restored his spirit, and allowed me to know who he was before his culture was destroyed. And I can see him, I can hear the coyotes, I can be among the women who "suddenly turned shy at dawn." Even if I hadn't studied indigenous cultures, lived among the people, I would still be at home because I have been invited in. There is a keen hospitality in Endrezze's work.

The poet's husband is Danish, and she was married in that country. On Midsummer's Eve in Denmark bonfires are lit on the beach and a witch/woman is burned in effigy. There she is experiencing both an old, old mystery, and her own passionate self,

I run into the hill of twilight this
passion burning deeper than my bones….
but I with my secret   eye
the strange light horned god moon O small
in the fields greening dance the fox musk
stink in my hair   I love it   the wild
man I can never trust

And this too is Now: Women attempting to recapture ritual, a wildness, a sensuality and aliveness in nature that so many societies have attempted to bury beneath constraint. I am at home with her "in the fields greening dance." I too know that "what husbands never know we never hide." It is rapture to read this midsummer dance of a poem. I am breathless when I finish.

In *Song of our Times*, the rapturous voice continues as she writes of her identification, her oneness with all that is alive, from the hot scented fox to the hunter polishing his gun. And she is one with all that we have imagined "the one living under the bridge of your fairy tale"…, and what has been made ugly - "the pitted-skin men at the end of the smokestack." And she is, finally,

> the land that was created from mud and put
> on a turtle's back,
> that fell from the sky, that was thrust from the
> roots,
> that was the heart of an Indian.

Now is a time of extinction. Woodland, marsh, desert, it doesn't matter - all can be inhabited by humans, taken over for development. In *Calypso*, the poet is still singing, but it is a lament, a psalm, for that rare, delicate endangered orchid, for all we are losing. She is searching for the *Calypso*, and knows she will recognize it at once: the full- magdalen lips, the magenta veil,

What follows is a series of metaphorical images for what she finds in the woods -

> friar gray
> wren scratches the bell-shaped pile
> of leaves.

- but we are not allowed to remain in a pristine wilderness. This is not Wordworth's or Frost's natural world, not W.S. Merwin's limpid, restored land, not Robert Hass's contented landscapes:

At our feet, the

> aluminum cans of poachers dazzle slugs.
> Chainsaw oil is the myrrh of moss.

And still the poem will shift and encompass ever higher powers. And the ending, which I will allow you to discover yourself, is an unanticipated surprise.

In *Calendars*, Endrezze leaves person and place for the measured abstraction of time. She tells us that there are many different calendars, that each substance, each symbol may have its own calendar, and "there is time enough for everything, they say," "the ice to keep time with the cracking of stars." Such mystery and actuality in that last image, for we are in fact the matter of exploded stars, and, in the words of Neil deGrasse Tyson, "we are also stardust in the highest most exalted way."

SONG MAKER

There is a drunk on Main Avenue, slumped
in front of the Union Gospel Mission.
He is dreaming of pintos the color of wine
and ice, and drums that speak the names
of wind. His hair hides his face,
but I think I know him.

Didn't he make songs people still sing
in their sleep?
Didn't coyotes beg him for new songs
to give to the moon?
Didn't he dance all night once and laugh
when the women suddenly turned
shy at dawn?
Didn't he make a song just for me,
one blessed by its being sung only once?

If he would lift his face
i could see his eyes, see
if he's singing now
a soul-dissolving song.
But he's all hunched over
and everyone walks around him.
He must still have strong magic
to be so invisible.

I remember him saying
Even grass has a song,
'though only wind hears it.

MIDSUMMER EVE

Denmark 1998
*On Midsummer's Eve, bonfires are built all over
Denmark. A witch/woman is burned in effigy.*

a man walks up a hill   red
knowing the way past the whirring
air the wind mills blade
there's no point in hurrying

from the poppies scarlet flood
or the people drinking coffee   stand
aside for the black trees   we wed
the old ways with ax, spade and

the sea like a horse's calm eye   glazed
with torch light gathering all the dark
shapes into one memory we gaze
at the one that is not us   chosen   walk

into the long twilight   hands
stack branches log over log
lighting the bonfires at the edge of the land
into the flames the rag-bone hag

couples walk into the hills birds
never sleep I remember waking
next to the man green or furred
his long tongue in one of my mouths   taking

I run into the hill of twilight this
passion burning deeper than my bones
what my husband never can miss
not having known

but I with my secret   eye
the strange light horned god   moon   O   small
sacrifices of life so slowly we die
meaning much to us or not at all

in the fields greening dance the fox musk
stink in my hair   I love it   the Wild
man I can never trust
what husbands never know   we never hide

the long uphill of the marriage bed   alone
fire upon wood, the spark that should breathe
light into each dark hour   what is known
every woman is midsummer eve

SONG OF OUR TIMES

I'm the dark water salmon, leaping
from the red-fleshed net of ancient dreams.
I'm the spotted trout,
the spaces between falling water.
I'm the only beach, the ragged wing of gull and tern,
the dead eye of the river.
I'm the stinking rain in your palm.

I'm the rough-barked tamarack,
the long-leafed willow.
I'm the animal without a face.

I'm the deep shadowed bear,
the windy-haired child.
I'm the crooked bones with eyes.
I'm the bandy-legged woman
with the third world hunger in your city.

I'm the tall, loose-limbed woman,
I'm the heron with tasseled reeds for bones,
I'm the mud-red salamander
the small bird of the moon.

I'm the one living under the bridge
of your fairy tale. I'm the warty frog of your tongue.
I'm the gray air of your love songs.
I'm the pitted-skin man at the end of the smokestack.

I'm the hill-breasted woman.
I'm the white tall deer with a song of cedar
curdled by the parasites in my throat.
I'm the snake that rides wild horses.

I'm the hot scented fox, the girl with blue sky
charms on her wrist and sunflowers in her hair.
I'm the baby sleeping under the mountain ash.
I'm the hunter polishing his gun,
the boy dancing in his baggy pants and semi-shaved head.
I'm the porcupine your mother warned you about,
the one with switchblade smiles and orange teeth.

I'm the bad-assed coyote sniffing at your sister.
I'm the wild butterflies in your lover's hands.
I'm the salmon he brings to you as a gift.
I'm the basket of sun she gives you one rainy day.

I'm the gangly bachelor button thriving in the ditch,
the summer ending like a long sleep in a slow swinging
hammock.
I'm the land that was created from mud and put
on a turtle's back,
that fell from the sky, that was thrust from the roots,
that was the heart of an Indian. I'm the song
that will never be finished.

CALYPSO

(an endangered woodland orchid)

As we search for rare orchids in the spring rain
let us light the candles of moonlight.
In our fingernails and face
the icons of wind and leaf.

We'll know the Calypso orchid instantly: the full-
magdalen lips, the magenta veil,
the absence of stones in nearby soil.
Endangered. Elusive. Female.

Under the burnt wick stems of buckthorn, a friar gray
wren scratches the bell-shaped pile
of leaves. Fiddlehead ferns tune
the misty air.

On the moist paths we make deep in the moss, there
are trilliums white-faced and holy.
Mute, they listen for the finger-
prints of wind.

Other trilliums, maroon, carrion-colored, wanton,
their faces turning to earth, confess
our secrets to the emissaries of flies.
There in the candelabra of clouds,
our prayers burn the ozone: make me rich,

make me pretty, make me powerful, make
me innocent.

We hope for a crown of pure air. We wait for an angel
robed in green ferns. At our feet, the
aluminum cans of poachers dazzle slugs.
Chainsaw oil is the myrrh of moss.

If we are made in God's image, let us imagine that our skin
is the plateau of Her breath,
our eyes the inner map of stars,
and our tongues the tongues of orchids,
our only testament the chime of rain on wings.

Not the polysyllables of toxins and polluted aquifers,
our bones just commas in cancerous flesh,
our skin a controversy of yellow rain
and bee shit, our blood an alphabet of pesticides,
our fingers like combs untangling the gray air,
our voices crying: Bless me, Bless me.

CALENDARS

the days are circles of bread, paper-words, the light in the egg
the nights are grass-moons, volcanic glass,
    the dark wine of the body
the calendars of water is lightening-flint, the dew that scars
    the iris, the bitter salt of blood

my wrist is time's turning on bone, the sinew of grace

the sky is an enormous shadow
over us all the eternal questions
whose shadow? whose time?

the calendar of stone is gold and sand, the blind eye
    of fossils, dust layered on cold water

the calendar of crosses depends on the sin of the wood
the calendar of sin depends on the carpenter's measure

the tongue seconds the loins, the heart beats
in the plum's falling, the pulse in the slender neck

there is time enough for everything, they say
time enough for orange to become red,
the November-colored hair to turn white,
the ice to keep time with the cracking of stars

the calendar of dawn is in the good-byes,
the lovers' last looks,
    the milky dream of thighs

the healing transforms the open wound
heart or skin, into moments of pure clarity

we know our mortal limits
thousands of leaves nest in the earth
we lay down our flesh for joy or death

the calendar of bones passes, unnoticed and obvious

Since I'm in *The Book of Now*, it's appropriate to start off by saying who I am now in my life. I am 60, a mother, wife, artist, writer, and I have MS. MS has defined my life these last dozen years. I try to work around it, standing up to paint in order to encourage circulation and muscle strength. I alternate writing with painting; my Now is full of painting. But my Now is also the publication of a new book of short stories, "Butterfly Moon" (U of Az press, 2012) written when I was in my full bore writing spree about 2 years ago. Because there have been times when my right hand was paralyzed, I take advantage of typing or painting when I can. I never know what tomorrow will bring.

Previous books include: "Throwing fire at the Sun, water at the Moon" (U of Az Press, 2000) and "at the helm of twilight" (Broken Moon Press 1992). Most recent chapbook of poems is "Breaking Edges" (Red Bird Press, 2012). For a somewhat complete bibliography and to see my visual art, go to

Endrezzeendrezze.weebly.com

LEAH SHELLEDA

*"Who will be called to
build an ark for rising waters?"*

I believe that life is sacred - all life. I could easily quote Keats here: *"that is all/ Ye know on earth, and all ye need to know,"* but then what would I write for the rest of this piece? And what about the second part "beauty is truth, truth beauty"? Had Keats not died so young he may have eventually learned that not all that is beautiful is true, and not all that is true is beautiful.

What is true for me? The waters are rising and the animals are dying. I dreamed that I had to name all the animals of the sixth extinction. I have always loved animals, since childhood. I have watched elephants tug an infant free of the mud in Africa. I have woken on a frigid India morning, wrapped myself in blankets, boarded a jeep, and seen tigers sitting like regents on the rocks above me. It is hard for me to bear that animals may only survive in books and photos and zoos. It is hard for me to not write yet one more poem, one more letter to my grandchildren lamenting the fact that I am not leaving them a sane, sustainable world.

> Dear grandchildren
> born into global warming
>   accelerating generations
>   separate us
> what I know of ice and snow   seasons
> the depth of water   all we counted on
> this knowledge will not be yours

The plight of the earth has taken my voice, and I dream of a new Noah, another drunkard, (In Genesis 9:20-25 Noah lands the ark, plants a vineyard, gets drunk off its wine), who is called to save us, and that unknown spirit entered *The Art Piece From Oaxaca*. It is the only myth that has come to me lately, though the stories and symbols of everyone from Mary Magdalen to Kitsune, the Japanese spirit fox, have infused my writing. I have exchanged myth for metamorphosis, as you will see in the poem with that word in its title, and - Warning! - I have a tendency to shape-shift mid verse.

Because I fell in love with Mother Goose, and began writing poems when I was 4, rhyme and rhythm and alliteration are automatic, and I must work against that natural tendency, lest it take over my poems. Not that I'm against form; but that my language must be freer, not meeting a demand for the right rhyme or repetition.

In *Extinct Birds* I allowed the rhyme and repetition to enter in order to evoke birdsong. (If only I could include one of the beautiful illustrations from the 1907 volume that provided the poem's title!)

> The violet macaw is beautiful
> but the sounds of 'spectacled cormorant'
> the hard 'c's' and rounded rhyming o's
> (say it slowly   c-o-r-m-o-r-a-n-t)
> launch me into language
> but
> on every page
> "No known specimen"

My poems are often inspired by other arts. The contemporary artist, Kiki Smith, who is continually metamorphosing among themes and arts and even crafts, has inspired several poems. But even in this poem that contains Smith's imagery -

> I saw a woman born of a doe
> I saw a woman step out of the body of a wolf
> There is return

a wounded Gaia appears and takes over the poem.

> Gaia I know you are wounded
> it is hard for you to breathe
> I dreamed you shed your scarred
> strip-mined surface
> and underneath was skin
> the pink of healing

I often write about the changes I see and feel in this country. As a cultural historian, I tend to look at even my own time from a 'birds-eye view,' or I try to delve into the collective to see what gods are in favor these post-industrial days. I find what is rising out of the remains of industrialism in this country remarkable. The photos of an American city in ruins have shocked and distressed, especially because I was raised in the time of its dynamism - but something new is happening there, and it took at least five different tries before I could find the form of *The New Land*, and the sound of the poem. How to mingle history and the present, how to use lengthy sentences for history and short phrases for Now; how to mix narrative and description:

> You've heard of that city
> It had an affair
> with concrete and steel
> the machine was their lovechild
> they named it Advance

and I don't want you to think any of that was a deliberate, conscious strategy, as though an academic is formatting her intellect. If each poem is not a new learning, a new experiment, it is not an adventure, and this aging poet still seeks adventure.

Neither my life, nor my poems are only a lament. In *Praise Song* I surprised myself by rising to rhapsody as I listed the multitudes that still remain - and at the moment of that writing I was the most blessed of women.

> I want tribes to sing
>> before they're unspoken
>>> I want us to sing for the sake of
> sound
>>>> birdsong   croak and
> cricket-creak

THE END OF ABUNDANCE

Dear grandchildren
born into global warming
   accelerating generations
         separate us
what I know of ice and snow   seasons
the depth of water   all we counted on
this knowledge will not be yours

I was born into war
sacrifice   rationing
you arrived at the end
of abundance

But who would rather remain unborn
     than enter a desperate age?

Little dear ones
time is a rope   twirled by invisible twin girls
we jump in
and skip
   for as long as we can

THE ART PIECE FROM OAXACA

Noah has arrived in my home
He stands next to the gangway
   of a carved wooden Ark
      mounted on a sculpture of scripture
His ship comes equipped with trumpeting angel
The four-footed push each other forward
the webbed and winged land on the tiled roof
land on the hived sides
     the ark fills
       antlers poke through portholes
When forty days of rain end
A rainbow encircles the ark
and the animals take color
hippos turn purple crows ultramarine coyotes orange

I think of faithful drunken Noah measuring the world in cubits
Who will be called to build an ark for the rising waters?
Some man some woman in a bar
may be mumbling their love for the animals
    awaiting word
When we walk past the art piece from Oaxaca
we bow our head to the trumpeting angel
and listen
just listen

METAMORPH ISING

for the artist Kiki Smith

Metamorphosis means more than once
as it is with egg larva pupa butterfly
as it is with some lives when larval stripes
and slow ripple are shed again and again
then comes the mimicry of dead leaf
till finally chrysalis splits and out flutters
wet-winged splendor

I saw a woman born of a doe
I saw a woman step out of the body of a wolf
There is return

Gaia I know you are wounded
it is hard for you to breathe
I dreamed you shed your scarred
strip-mined surface
and underneath was skin
the pink of healing
Now you must rest
and all of us wolf doe
woman man become pupa
In our silk cocoons
we wait   suspended

"EXTINCT BIRDS"

by Walter Rothschild   1907
illustrated by J. G. Keulemans

The violet macaw is beautiful
but the sounds of 'spectacled cormorant'
the hard 'c's' and rounded rhyming o's
(say it slowly   c-o-r-m-o-r-a-n-t)
launch me into language
but
on every page
"No known specimen"

I'm grounded
trying to find the alphabet
of lost flight
"No known specimen"

The Great Auk   the Madagascar hawk
the last ones died of indifference
Now the mere rumor of a remote
sighting would thrill us

If we didn't ignore
all but our own music
would the Carolina parakeet
still be singing?

The lyrebird
can mimic any sound   perfectly

The call of kookaburra currawong
the fall of a branch the click of a camera
Listen: his latest sound
      a chain saw

THE NEW LAND

You've heard of that city
It had an affair
with concrete and steel
the machine was their lovechild
they named it Advance
and how could it not
be the future?
That city was my first home
 Have you heard it's in ruins?
Next to 40 stories of abandoned smashed-glass skyscraper
and the startled remains of a Beaux-Arts station where
the 20th Century Limited pulled in and men and women
in hats and suits hired porters in perfectly shined shoes
Next to that
     long blocks of empty lots
I've been gone too long to know how the day-to-day goes
But it's a Black city now no supermarkets settle in
and nothing fresh comes from a liquor store
So the women go to the vacant spaces clean up the shards
the bullets the needles
hoe plow weed seed and feed the ground that belongs
to no one put in tomatoes corn greens potatoes
And the earth knows they are listening
says "Barter" says "Seed exchange" says "Saturday market"

Outside of the churches   among the early sprouts

they say prayers for the crop   grandaddy's hymn and Gaia hip-hop

arms reaching not skyward

but down

toward the rich reconsecrated land

of Detroit

PRAISE SONG

I want to sing the life of the earth
an egg   a nest   a hive   the herd
uncountable wings in the wet forest
microbes thriving in the heat of a geyser
the unknown swimming the canyons of the sea
what the cat scans as she stalks the savannah
what the hunter sees as he moves through the veldt
the invisible in a bead of water

I want to sing the profusion of peoples
Camel-riding desert Tuareg draped in blue
Balinese balancing edible towers
The last Hazda drilling fire
Inuit curving snow blocks into dome
   the stunning variety of indigenous homes
      the bo-sa a house of bamboo   adobe   hogan   igloo
I want to sing the children on their way to the temple
      mosque   pagoda   kiva   jinja
    I want tribes to sing
     before they're unspoken
       I want us to sing for the sake of sound
        birdsong croak and cricket-creak
Praise all I have named   this relic
        residue

    remnant

  remainder

Leah Shelleda is Professor Emeritus of Humanities and Philosophy at the College of Marin. Her poems have appeared in many journals and anthologies, and her chapbook, *A Flash of Angel,* won the Blue Light Press Prize. Her recent book of poetry, *After the Jug Was Broken,* was published by Fisher King Press. Leah is a gardener, a weaver, a lifetime seeker and a crone-in-training.

CRYSTAL GOOD

"Mourning, good morning. Momma got work to do."

"To those who taught me how to drive" is the epigraph for *Valley Girl*. What if it is so hard to get out, to go somewhere, to realize your dream, and you manage to get out, get a degree, publish a book of poems, but you haven't left your roots, your people. Your name is Crystal Good, and you're from West Virginia, and the coal-driven life:

> Them boys say West Virginia girls are gold diggers
> Them boys should know better.
> 'Cause in West Virginia -
> there ain't no gold, just **black, black coal.**

I hear music in every phrase. For the spoken word poets, it's not other poets, past or present who are major influences, but the music they grew up with, the music they listen to. I asked Good about her music: "Lynard Skynard and Public Enemy growing up, but also Madonna, Cindy Lauper and Tupac. I listen to neo soul/ R&B, Bill Withers (from WV) and hip-hop (Outcast, Nas, Common)." Ummmhmmmm.

On yet untouched sections of the Appalachian Trail, back-packers seek peace, but in West Virginia there is none. They're still digging, sending men down, down to the tortured rock, coming back up with black lungs. And now they also blow the top off mountains with mountain-high equipment - Good might say you haven't seen big until you've been there- Think of those blown mountains, god knows what toxins leaking into the groundwater, babies born with defects. Good is the voice of those people, and she's the voice of the mountains, and its not only a vernacular voice, a hip-hop voice, a "Quantum Christian" voice, but a pagan one. It might be that "The Road to Redemption runs through West Virginia" with a church at every crossroads, but Mountain Mama is a living being, the earth is alive in these poems and isn't it all about penetration?

> Holding her breath, she let him go in
> gentle, like before the other Jaspers came.
> He drilled deeper and deeper

"Jasper," not incidentally, means outsider in Southern Appalachian/Smokey Mountain dialect. "Mountain Mama" means that the eternal feminine has emerged in West Virginia, and her voice is direct and raw.

Raw emotion might make for power, deep feeling is powerful, but it takes something else to make a poem. You need a distinctive voice, engagement, an inner voice that speaks to you, and craft: Original language and imagery that take you to new places. Some fine poems are closer to vision, and some closer to music. And then there's Good. Her poems unite deep feeling to sound and imagery. That music comes from deep inside the mountain, so deep "them boys" can't reach it.

This "Valley Girl" moves around, and when she travels to New England she meets (and there is no better word) the paper birch tree and the love is there and the fact of it - "the peeling, shedding itself, vulnerable." There is always just a bit of irony of humor, a dont-think-my-observing-eye-didn't-pick-this-up says the Affriliachen amid the prettiness of New England.

> I had never seen anything like it,

never been here in this part of the country
with a wilderness behind a security gate.

But Mountain WildOne emerges here

Man stroking back and forth, back and forth.
Holding my stare, watching his turn to breath,
kiss the air.
Knowing only, this temptation was great.

Ummmhmmmm. Mountain WildOne doesn't say no to temptation, takes the risks that intense pleasure requires, and by the end of the poem Good has bonded with that shedding, peeling, vulnerable birch and Mountain Mama, protective of her own says:

Leave it alone
That's my tree

Crystal Good is dedicated to the people of West Virginia, and not just because it says so on the back cover of her book. Her dedication is alive in the poems and in her service to the community. She is Vice President of Create West Virginia - a grassroots initiative to build the new, creative economy of WV. Sure she's a college graduate, she knows Quantum Physics, she knows that light can be both wave and particle, (you can be both the next wave and a part of your people) - but it's a balancing act. You may become moss, as she does in one of her poems, preferring shade, able to adapt to urban conditions, without roots, but you cannot survive in polluted air. Grystal Good is the next generation.

In *WV Mourning*, Good laments The Upper Big Branch Mine Disaster, April 5, 2010. 29 men out of the 32 working the mine lost their lives after an explosion. The mine owners were faulted for lack of safety measures. 500 citations had already been issued for violations.

We'll let Mountain Mama respond:

She is
Wearing resilience and tears like stickers on a hard hat.
She wakes the children. Get up. Get up.
Mourning, good morning. Momma got work to do.

BOOM BOOM

Them boys say West Virginia girls are gold diggers
Them boys should know better.
'Cause in West Virginia -
there ain't no gold, **just black, black coal.**

Them girls them West Virginia girls -
don't take no handouts - **they got a living
to make - strippin' is hard work.**

Everyday, they get high - on three million pounds
pretending not to notice - their bodies change.
They wait/prepare.

A concubine of wild mountains orchids
grooming landing strips - for them **hometown
millionaires to fly in** - then **sell - them out**
always reminding them, **they really not worth much.**

Them boys come back 'round after all the damage
is done. After all her long hair is gone. They grin/admire
what's left of her hips - just checkin' on you.

Them girls them silly girls just smile any attention will do.
They wait they prepare getting ready burning tan lines in

layers deep -
until the music begins.

BOOM! BOOM!
Them boys like that bass loud.

BOOM! BOOM!
Them girls shake it.

BOOM! BOOM!
Them girls dance.

They bend over taking tips in G-stream drunk on slurry
holding up their middle finger - thumb out in a West Virginia
shape.
They shout- damn right we lookin' for a come up!
Where else we got to go/ 49th in America's list of opportunity.

Them boys like it when them girls talk back.
They say they like 'em a little wild a little wonderful
smack their ass watch them girls tumble down.

Them boys know some of the West Virginia girls can't count
Not 8 +1 or 2x2 they laugh calling them names **crazy - whore**
Just after they take all their mineral rights.

Them boys leave again, off to NASCAR gone fishing out of
state charity golf for the abused. They court Miss Kentuckys
smoke cigars sitting on top of them prettier West Virginia girls
the ones with not so many scars they ones they build mansions
on.

Them girls them West Virginia girls done lost all their dignity. They can't see no way out no right of way. They wonder if it's too late to get a **boob job** acrylic nails **new pair of platform shoes.**

Them girls them West Virginia girls don't take no handouts **They got a living to make**. So they keep on waving at them boys in Escalades, but them boys already reached inside, took what's of value.

Them boys just drive past never looking up or over just down at them West Virginia girls. Them girls cry hardest when the rain falls cause mudslides toxic messes in her mine, this is what she deserved.

Them boys say West Virginia girls are gold diggers.

Them boys should know better. **'Cause in West Virginia there ain't no gold, just black, black coal.**

Them boys. Them girls. Just keep on blasting the same song…

BOOM! BOOM! She was wrong.

BOOM BOOM! **FOREVER GONE.**

BOOM! BOOM!

Them girls.   Them mountains.   Explode.

PASSING WRONG

The Road to Redemption - runs through West Virginia. Tunnels
carry Old Regular hymn/tolls - fight past
church marquees - tombstones

Road side markets of screwdrivers- stuffed unicorns Valley
two-lanes warn -
> **falling rock**

Casting eyes of
atonement -
> **hanging**

Scenic overlooking holy fields. Courage washing traveler's feet
clean in pot holes. Winding the hallows of moments
rescued -
> **bloody**
> **blooming**
> **truth**

IN NEW ENGLAND

Batula Papyrilera (Paper Birch)

It was peeling, shedding itself, vulnerable.
Like it was coming to
the end of a season,
ready to transform.

I had never seen anything like it,
never been here in this part of the country
with a wilderness behind a security gate.
I wanted to know what its skin felt like.

Was it rough like a beard or smooth,
like a New River rock?
Why did it curl its self-back,
why did it want to leave?

Writer poets must document these memories.
Must tell the world when they see mermen
swimming in New England.
Must describe how they walk

In the water wearing fruit of da' looms
looking like a bearded Jesus, baptizing

and then morphing themselves.
They must tell the tenacity of lap,

after lap after lap in a decorated pool.
I count - the trees, the branches,
look at the grass full of scraps
and shred of empty swings.

Man stroking back and forth, back and forth.
Holding my stare, watching his turn to breath, kiss the air.
Knowing only, this temptation was great.
That I have long had this fetish for pulp,
of wanting to touch it, smell it, taste it
sometimes delicate and raw, recycled.
I collect it to create.

Pulling myself back to see through as man emerge long with legs
and feet - wet.
Standing close - to feel the drip,
pointing to the wood.
I feel the tremble in this Triton's growl,
watching him spin a towel and deliver the sting.

Leave it alone.
That's my tree.

WV MOURNING

It was a job, just work then Jasper
paused to tell her she was valuable

a hot mountain brown suga mama,
smart

Pretty was common, but smart
was sexy. She ignored safety.

Drunk on expensive martinis
he was greedy to fill her holler

speaking quietly - protection wasn't
necessary - helping her strip

out of her skin - taking off her mask,
production moved faster and faster.

Promises of more and more but
this wasn't love, her eyes never left the ground.

She handed him piece after piece showing off
her capable sides, letting him look at her

wild and wonderful tattoo- her Chessie Cat.
Jasper talked politics and promises

a big business hustler with a tongue
talented enough to spin her tall tail.

I will be good to you' I can take care of you
that will never happen to you,

Holding her breath, she let him go in
gentle, like before the other Jaspers came.

He drilled deeper and deeper than the explosion
first above then underground.

Mountain Mama had a history of violations
sirens, sounded, emergency in the dark

Twenty feet below ground in a carpeted rec room
she tries to digest the news, but she can't move.

Sleeping with a prayer this time will be
different. She wakes with another broken heart.

Wearing resilience and tears like stickers on a hard hat.
She wakes the children. Get up. Get up.

Mourning, good morning. Momma got work to do.

Crystal Good is a writer poet living in West Virginia with her three sons. Her first chapbook of poetry, *Valley Girl*, explores themes in quantum physics, Appalachian culture, gender equality and mountaintop removal. Printed in 2012, the book quickly became as classroom resource at James Madison University and the University of Kentucky.

Her work has been called "dazzling, bold, innovative, disarming." Jeff Biggers of The Huffington Post says Good's poetry "wonderfully carries on the legacy of (her) fellow 'Affrilachian Poets' including the spellbinding work of recent National Book Award-winning poet Nikky Finney and Frank X. Walker."

She is published in Pluck! The Journal for Affrilachian Culture and Appalachian Heritage.

DUNYA MIKHAIL

"Life is a handful of nails in the hand of a shoemaker."

When I encountered her poems, I sent the following message to Dunya Mikhail:

> Dear Keeper of the Flame,
>
> I have read and wept over your poems - and been relieved. Relieved? How could I be relieved? Because a woman is writing of war in her own imagery, in her own voice, and most significantly, these are poems that can encompass all modern warfare, wherever it is waged.

Dunya Mikhail witnessed dictatorship and war in Iraq. She was forced to leave her country and go into permanent exile in the United States. Mikhail's Arabic anti-war writings had incited the Iraqi authorities, and the harassment could no longer be borne. When will they just imprison or kill you? She loathes the glorification of war, and laments the torture, the raped, the dead. "The gods are bored," she says in one poem, "they are ignoring us."

In the title poem of her book, *The War Works Hard*, Mikhail's voice is ironic - she stands back from the horror, and describes all that war is able to accomplish:

> Early in the morning,
> it wakes up the sirens

and dispatches ambulances
to various places,

swings corpses through the air,
rolls stretchers to the wounded,

and she tells of medals awarded to generals, the artificial limb industry flourishing. As she describes all that war does, all that it "accomplishes," the reader has a true understanding of how war takes over an entire society; an entire life. Mikhail's translator describes her voice as "child-like," but I never knew a child with the simultaneous detachment and sorrow that I find in this poem. Or others. Some of the rhythms and repetitions remind me of both the Psalms and Arabic poetry.

Dunya Mikhail is a witness - and a Courier. The Couriers witnesses injustice and evil. They can spell out at least a few of the secret names that evil takes. Their words are lanterns held up to what has been secretly or illegally accomplished; to what a country, a society wants to hide. Often, the Couriers have been poets. We are blessed to have these Couriers, many of them great poets like Celan, Mandelstam, Trakl & Appolinaire. And now there is Dunya Mikhail.

One of Mikhail's gifts is the ability to take on a variety of voices. In *The Prisoner* she speaks as the mother of a political prisoner:

It never occurred to her,
as she sang lullabies on his bed
in those distant days,
someday, he would end up in this cold place
without windows or moons.

The language is so precise, as she contrasts the warmth of his infancy with "this cold place." A place without windows or moons. Without an opening, without the feminine, the mother.

In *Bag of Bones*, she is in the boneyard, among what remains. And from her own depths, she brings us a stunning and original image in the same precise language:

> To give back to your mother
> on the occasion of death
> a handful of bones
> she had given to you
> on the occasion of birth?

But this poem is more than a lament. Later, she will give us the dictator who is responsible for this tragedy, though he does not bear it alone,

> he has an audience, too,
> an audience that claps
> until the bones begin to rattle -

In *I Was In A Hurry*, Mikhail writes about the initial experience of exile, of fleeing, of being so caught up in the process, the movement, that only later does she realize that:

> Yesterday I lost a country.
> I was in a hurry,
> and I didn't notice when it fell from me
> like a broken branch from a forgetful tree.

The twentieth and twenty first century have been a time of massive exile. 1,400,000 Iraqi refugees were uprooted as a result of the Persian Gulf War (1990–91). The United Nations estimated that nearly 5,000,000 refugees fled the country since

2003, when The U.S. army arrived to "save" it. Yes, you read it right: 5,000,000 refugees.

I once wrote

> This century of exile   the last century of exile
> someone maybe you is always forced to leave
> to go where your language is not spoken
> to hide in the crowded quarter of your dialect
> where your word for bread is their word
> and laughter is a cousin
>
> you will speak of absent trees   flowers
> that will not bloom foods you cannot swallow
> you are too dark or too light for this country

In *The Shoemaker* and *The Jewel*, the poet uses the commonplace and the precious as different metaphors for life, each coming to a different conclusion - each equally valid, holding the opposites between them.

May her home-in-exile nurture Mikhail's poetry. May the saints of the Christian community she was raised in intercede on her behalf. May the spirit of Sumerian Inanna, she who presides over love and fertility, she who descended into the Underworld and returned, watch over her.

THE WAR WORKS HARD

How magnificent the war is!
How eager
and efficient!
Early in the morning,
it wakes up the sirens
and dispatches ambulances
to various places,
swings corpses through the air,
rolls stretchers to the wounded,
summons rain
from the eyes of mothers,
digs into the earth
dislodging many things
from under the ruins…
Some are lifeless and glistening,
others are pale and still throbbing…
It produces the most questions
in the minds of children,
entertains the gods
by shooting fireworks and missiles
into the sky,
sows mines in the fields
and reaps punctures and blisters,
urges families to emigrate,
stands beside the clergymen
as they curse the devil
(poor devil, he remains

with one hand in the searing fire)…
The war continues working, day and night.
It inspires tyrants
to deliver long speeches,
awards medals to generals
and themes to poets.
It contributes to the industry
of artificial limbs,
provides food for flies,
adds pages to the history books,
achieves equality
between killer and killed,
teaches lovers to write letters,
accustoms young women to waiting,
fills the newspapers
with articles and pictures,
builds new houses
for the orphans,
invigorates the coffin makers,
gives grave diggers
a pat on the back
and paints a smile on the leader's face.
The war works with unparalleled diligence!
Yet no one gives it
a word of praise.

THE PRISONER

She doesn't understand
what it means to be "guilty."
She waits at the prison entrance
until she sees him, to say,
"Take care of yourself,"
as she always used to remind him
when he went off to school
when he left for work,
when he returned on vacation.
She doesn't understand
what they are saying now
at the back of the podium
in their official uniforms.
They report that he should be kept there
with lonely strangers.
It never occurred to her,
as she sang lullabies on his bed
in those distant days,
someday, he would end up in this cold place
without windows or moons.
She doesn't understand,
the prisoner's mother doesn't understand
why she should leave him
just because
"The visit is over."

BAG OF BONES

What good luck!
She has found his bones.
The skull is also in the bag
the bag in her hand
like all other bags
in all other trembling hands.
His bones, like thousands of bones
in the mass graveyard,
His skull, not like any other skull.
Two eyes or holes
with which he saw too much,
two ears
with which he listened to music
that told his own story,
a nose
that never knew clean air,
a mouth, open like a chasm,
it was not like that when he kissed her
there, quietly,
not in this place
noisy with skulls and bones and dust
dug up with questions:
What does it mean to die all this death
in a place where the darkness plays all this silence?
What does it mean to meet your loved ones now
With all of these hollow places?
To give back to your mother

on the occasion of death
a handful of bones
she had given to you
on the occasion of birth?
To depart without death or birth certificates
because the dictator does not give receipts
when he takes your life.
The dictator has a skull too,
a huge one.
It solved by itself a math problem
that multiplied the one death by millions
to equal homeland.
The dictator is the director of a great tragedy.
he has an audience, too,
an audience that claps
until the bones begin to rattle -
the bones in the bags,
the full bag finally in her hand,
unlike her disappointed neighbor
who has not yet found her own.

TRAVEL AGENCY

A pile of travelers is on the table.
Tomorrow their planes will take off
and dot the sky with silver
and descend like evening on the cities.
Mr. George says that his beloved
no longer smiles at him.
He wants to travel directly to Rome
to dig a grave there like her smile.
"But not all roads lead to Rome," I remind him,
and hand him a ticket for one.
He wants to sit by the window
to be sure that the sky
is the same
everywhere.

I WAS IN A HURRY

Yesterday I lost a country.
I was in a hurry,
and I didn't notice when it fell from me
like a broken branch from a forgetful tree.
Please, if anyone passes by
and stumbles across it,
perhaps in a suitcase
open to the sky,
or engraved on a rock
like a gaping wound,
or wrapped
in the blankets of emigrants,
or canceled
like a losing lottery ticket,
or helplessly forgotten
in Purgatory,
or rushing forward without a goal
like the questions of children,
or rising with the smoke of war,
or rolling in a helmet on the sand,
or stolen in Ali Baba's jar,
or disguised in the uniform of a policeman
who stirred up the prisoners
and fled,
or squatting in the mind of a woman
who tries to smile,
or scattered

like the dreams
of new immigrants in America.
If anyone stumbles across it,
return it to me, please.
It is my country…
I was in a hurry
when I lost it yesterday.

SHOEMAKER

A skillful shoemaker
throughout his life
he has pounded the nails
and smoothed the leather
for a variety of feet:
feet that depart
feet that kick
feet that plunge
feet that pursue
feet that run
feet that trample
feet that collapse
feet that jump
feet that trip
feet that are still
feet that tremble
feet that dance
feet that return...
Life is a handful of nails
in the hand of a shoemaker.

THE JEWEL

It no longer stretches across the river.
It is not in the city,
not on the map.
The bridge that was...
The bridge that we were...
The Pontoon Bridge
we crossed every day...
Dropped by the war into the river
just like the blue jewel
that lady dropped
off the side of the Titanic.

Dunya Mikhail, Iraqi-American poet, was born in Baghdad in 1965 and left Iraq to the US (Michigan) in mid 1990s. She has worked as a journalist for "The Baghdad Observer" and her work was found "subversive." She was awarded the UN Human Rights Award for Freedom of Writing in 2001, and her translator, Elizabeth Winslow, won a 2004 Pen Translation Fund Award. Her first book in English, *The War Works Hard* (New Directions 2005, Carcanet 2006) was shortlisted for the Griffin Prize and was named one of the 25 books to remember in 2005 by the New York Public Library. It was also translated into Italian by Elena Chiti and published by Edizioni San Marco dei Giustiniani (Rome, 2011). *Mikhail's Diary of A Wave Outside the Sea* (New Directions, NY, 2009) won the 2010 Arab American Book Award.

FRANCES HATFIELD

"When it rains I remember
we are married to our secrets"

There are writers who give the world to us in stark terms - they look at the evil, the pain of modern life, spit in pity's eye and rhyme the dark corner they inhabit in time to a blast or a naked dirge.

Frances Hatfield is a poet who has no fear of depths or ugliness or disease, but she insists on cloaking what she discovers in skillfully crafted, if not beautiful, language. The words are wrought iron, so the craft does not prettify. Instead it removes any ambiguity, and she doesn't allow you to back away from her subject and simply revel in metaphor. She has invited us into her interiority, and we enter to discover unburied treasure.

We are a generation who seem to be almost obsessed with wellness, with self-care. A thousand approaches, and thousands of practitioners proliferate, each with special claims.

In Hinduism, those who are willing to undertake the most difficult path practice Rajah Yoga, and those who are willing to undertake the most challenging form of therapy choose Jungian or Freudian-based analysis. You must become a tracker, tracking your own path backwards, and you will encounter such pain and resistance, such monsters - but your insight will slowly grow, healing is possible, and you will create a symbolic universe of your own.

Hatfield is a psychologist, and a candidate at the Jung Institute of San Francisco. She has been a tracker herself, and now she follows the tracks of others, and never have I read poetry that described 'The Work' more accurately. But accuracy alone, without the symbolic, the precise imagery, the willingness to evoke terror, would not have created *The Talking Cure:*

> Tracking bloody prints
> through halls of mirrored fractals
> down broken trails of memory
> of church basement—nursery—
> sewer—crypt, by the time
> you know the real reason you came
> it's too late

In *Rough Guide to the Underworld*, Hatfield becomes our Homer, our Dante, our Guide, writing not the Other World, but the inner one "where all that you are or ever have been is reduced to the weight of a nickel." She describes what you will experience, and the new skills you will attain: Walls won't stop you, and "now you remember you could always fly." Not that the underworld is a pleasing, inviting place: In *The Talking Cure* she informed us that "the snarls of the guard dogs hang like icicles in the air." Finally, her tone shifts to humor, and in *Rough Guide to the Underworld* you will learn why "the great god Pluto cannot just ask a girl out for a date."

Since I am committed to holding the opposites, I must mention the other side of wellness - a scourge of pollution, of toxic chemicals, of child asthma - and an epidemic of breast cancer. That too is Now. Perhaps we are obsessed with wellness because there appear to be such threats to health. Hatfield has facilitated a group of women with breast cancer, and she writes about them with marvelous flexibility: She relies on the imagery of ancient myth in *Monday Night Cancer Group*, but in *Just Like A Woman* she launches into a tell-it-like-it-is down home song of "audacious" women living large through chemo, radiation - up to the worst:

> Wouldn't you guess Linda might
> steal out between rounds of radiation & chemo
> her body on fire, her bones ice
> to plant a cornfield
> in her backyard

We have such histories in our times. Many treatments, loves, multiple marriages, lives that shift and change cities, countries, careers. We may try to forge a life without custom or community, or create a virtual one on social media. Many are self-exiles who never arrive.

But Now is also forever - the forever of the soul. A rainy night, a bird calling, lover asleep in her bed and the shape of a name moves his lips - and the bird and the unnamed together bring her to a reverie on the delicacy of the heart - and the arcs and circles and curves of *The Soul's Geometry*.

And as we began Hatfield's journey into deep, dimensional space, so we end there.

> We are not traveling a straight line as thoughts do.
> A circle is a line that went looking for itself.

THE TALKING CURE

Tracking bloody prints
through halls of mirrored fractals
down broken trails of memory
of church basement—nursery—
sewer—crypt, by the time
you know the real reason you came
it's too late

the locked gate to the forbidden
room gapes open
the snarls of the guard dogs
hang like icicles in the air
and the array of weaponry that once
worked so well, turns out
to be cardboard, a set prop
for a war drama that has no beginning
and may have no end

and we know words are the least of it,
flimsy souvenirs of the vast
catacombs of the heart
opening between us
week after week, mere
bubbles rising to the surface
while our bodies breathe and gesture

through portals of sunken ships
still pointing towards Ithaca,
cargo intact, flags waving
as if time didn't matter
as if the lost and the dead
were not.

ROUGH GUIDE TO THE UNDERWORLD

It's not just for the dead, it's not heaven or hell,
but if you've made it this far, you know that.
You notice at once how everything is almost
the opposite of what you expected.
The world you left is not left, there's really no under or after:

Between the molecules of your life, in the interstitial seas
of its bursting forth and withering,
in each offbeat of your heart,
world upon world unfurls and vanishes,
moving to a clock whose tick lasts an aeon,
yet feels like an instant, where all that you are
or ever have been is reduced to the weight of a nickel.

Now you find you can walk through walls
you once knew simply as "myself,"
and now you remember you could always fly,
except now your body's a vast school of small fish,
and you speak in an alphabet of light and motion

with the dream bodies of the living and the dead
who are never dead, who flit or grind or whisper
through us decade after decade,

and there on the floor, all you ditched
in this life to stay afloat, that just seemed too big,
too hard, only garbage, or worse,

revealed at this depth to be precious
and splendid beyond all telling.

and you realize: this is what your lovers glimpsed
that made them want to dive into you over and over,
gasping and crying out,
how many lifetimes we all spend trying to do this,
and you see now, too, why it never works for long,
atom by atom we float back up,
the rubies and diamonds, again just barnacles and rocks,

and now that you know what it costs to journey here
and even if you'd choose it again and again,
it becomes quite clear why the great god Pluto
cannot just ask a girl out for a date,

because who, on a spring day, knee-deep in green,
swaying in the perfume of narcissus and violets,
would willingly step into a marriage such as this,
who would pay a dowry of that nickel,
what girl on earth will say
Yes.

MONDAY NIGHT CANCER GROUP

One by one
and each alone
will sink down like Inanna
through the seven gates of hell,

lose the strapless dress,
mascara and pearls at the first gate,
then the hair, along with
all the rules and props, friendly
fictions, and of course
the dignities

and so on down
to the final ghastly gate
where all joy departs,
and the syllables of her lovely name
dissolve like sugar

naked and alone
she will look the terrible hag
straight in the eye
call her sister

while the rest of us wait
as women have always waited:
we light candles,

bring supper to dazed lovers and children,
picket the gates of the gods
for her return

JUST LIKE A WOMAN

Wouldn't you guess Linda might
steal out between rounds of radiation & chemo
her body on fire, her bones ice
to plant a cornfield
in her backyard

& isn't it just like Julie to remark
"I'm dying—
but it's not as bad as you think"

& leave it to that low down brazen hussy Gina
to strip down to this naked goose-pimpled moment
& expose her radiance
for everyone to see

& it takes one audacious woman
to fly in the face of public opinion
& give birth to herself
well past menopause

& you would expect some uppity women
who've lost careers and body parts and lovers
to keep churning beauty

out of potting wheels,
paintbrushes, sewing machines,
thin air

& isn't it just typical of one bald-headed
one-breasted woman
after another
to go around
spilling out life
like it was water

THE SOUL'S GEOMETRY

Rain seeps
into all the tired roots
pools in the locked-up souls of my city.
I stand in the doorway late at night
and listen. One bird calls, clear
and long, unmuffled by light. My lover sleeps.
I do not move, wanting to hear it
again. Its cry is the shape of a seahorse,
the curve of a wave reaching out of itself.
I have cried like that.

He sleeps and the shape of a name
moves his lips. When it rains I remember
we are married to our secrets
and all that we own grows out of the dark.
The unclaimed and the hidden,
the not yet and the ones left behind,
still live in the rain,
in the countries we have walked and dreamed of walking,
whose maps are carved on the palms of our hands,
and on vast islands of grief,
where our drowned footprints reappear
so far from each other.
We are not traveling a straight line as thoughts do.
A circle is a line that went looking for itself.

When it rains I remember
how delicate the curve of the heartline on the hand,
its branches and feathers, crosses and vanishings.
My heart could steal back to its castle of ghosts.
He could go again hunting with his wound and his bow.

Out of the arch of its cry
another bird comes, and answers.
I imagine how they find each other
somewhere under the eaves.

Frances Hatfield grew up in Western Louisiana, East Texas, and New Mexico, and now lives on the central coast of California, where she practices as a psychotherapist. She is the recipient of a UC Poet Laureate Award, and her work has appeared in numerous journals. Her book, *Rudiments of Flight*, was published by Wings Press in 2012.

JANE DOWNS

"It is a time when the wind upsets the gate,
the door blows open and the candle flares."

Beauty and terror. Holding the opposites. Not either/or but both-and. Gaia's beauty, the stars' glamour, the transcendence of art, the elegant lope of the giraffe. And terror - war, famine, melting glaciers, child soldiers, serial killers. It is the combination of loveliness and menace, the condition of Now, that attracted me to Jane Downs' poems.

Downs' has a special gift: The ability to bring to the surface what she experienced as a child, written in the simple, declarative sentences a child might use - but we never mistake her voice for a small person's. Her exquisite word choice leaves out all but the essential, and a child does not edit. In *The Weight of Pink Peonies* there is no metaphor , no analogy. An article flavors a sentence: The child cannot touch the baby rabbits, because not Mother, or my mother, but "the mother" will vanish at the smell. Her mother tells her things that announce madness, or physical illness. Everything is alive - "peonies crawl from a vase." There is menace. It is Now - but the poet has shown us a wound out of which this poem is written. Pleasure? "Sweet grass scent" and open air.

But in *To Katherine*, "daylight is too specific," grass, sky, "red red roses." It is a time when wind upsets the gates - a season? someone in crisis? Both/and? We don't know who Katherine is, though she is referred to as "child." Another of the poet's identities? A younger version of The Mother? It is "the night" that the poet invites Katherine into - darkness will reveal, and Katherine will not be distracted by what is "too specific." What we don't know, at least in this case, will not detract, will not hinder. There is a mystery here, and complexity. The poet has left room for your imagination, trusting you to find your way to her intent.

We enter the labyrinth in *The Minotaur.* I was in awe of this poem, the first of Downs' that I read. The creature is "Born from dark lake into fractured light, man pulled from skin of animal." In the original myth Passiphae, the wife of Minos, the Cretan ruler, and a great bull, come together, and she gives birth to a dangerous monster.

So many associations come to mind at once - David Abrams *"Becoming Animal."* The queen's alleged lust for the bull in mythology. Couldn't this be rape, as it was with the other gods who descend to earth to pursue and force a woman? The monster "beats against a wall of earth." It, he, He - knows what he is and suffers. But what of our own obscenity?

> Right now, a soldier kicks down a door,
> drags a woman from her bed
>
> Look, how beautiful from above,
> Each bomb a flower of smoke

And the woman will give birth. As women do who suffer rape, by a relative, a stranger, a soldier. Nothing new, nothing the world hasn't always experienced, only Now it is not hidden, not a secret shame, we know the truth. We learned it in Bosnia, in Rwanda, other parts of Africa, in documentaries, in middle class homes in America. At least, in the rare case that a perpetrator is brought to trial in this country, he can no longer say that we asked for it, that we'd done it with other men. "Ashes on her forehead. Ashes on her tongue."

> Downs' *Spring* is not peace and bloom and
> nesting birds.
> Listen to the restlessness
> of lilacs. Do you hear the way
> the river rushes
> by, the earth falling
> into the running
> water.

In the next stanza "Trains rattle/east to stock yards."

> That Spring. The sky shines benevolence, the
> lovers love - but beneath the earth there is
> something else, something much darker.

This is where the poem takes me: They look like ordinary days, this spring, this summer. Flowers, berries, the blue sky that says all is easy - but some of us cannot fool ourselves into "normal," even with the season's connivance. Though we blight the planet, still She tries to do her work, but we are closing in on tipping point, the waters are rising.

> "beneath us a god roams with dirt in his mouth."

THE WEIGHT OF PINK PEONIES

Cut grass smells sweeter than uncut. A nest of newborn rabbits under the lawn. I ache to touch one, know my scent would banish the mother. How careful I must be. There are abandoned nests on the porch. My mother says her hair is falling out. Says she has flies in her eyes. Open the door. Enter the house. Peonies crawl from a vase. I've outgrown the sleeveless pink dress. Mother sits on her hands. When she cuts peonies she wears rubber gloves. Open the window, lean on the ledge. Sweet grass scent, scrape of the mower blades. How careful I must be.

TO KATHERINE

It is a time when the wind upsets the gate,
the door blows open and the candle flares.

Open your eyes, child. Open your pale eyes.

The colors of the world devour the familiar
black of sky & white of moon.

Daylight is too specific. So much glistening grass,
cerulean sky and, oh, those red red roses. The brown
of the hare who runs from the hounds, the hawk's golden eye.

It is the night with its variegated blacks you must love.
Against the dark you can see your thoughts. Against the dark
a woman is more bone than flesh and stars more fierce.

THE MINOTAUR

Born from dark lake into fractured light,
man pulled from skin of animal

It beats against a wall of earth,
its head a helmet it would shatter

Grievous child, wrapped in labyrinthine lace
The woman mourns her monstrous child

How to banish our own obscenity.
Put a rope around its neck, corral it in a maze

Right now, a soldier kicks down a door,
drags a woman from her bed

Look, how beautiful from above,
each bomb a flower of smoke

Look, the molten river streaming,
houses paper stars in flames

Ashes on her forehead. Ashes on her tongue.
The woman weeps her child into this world

SPRING

Listen to the restlessness
of lilacs. Do you hear the way
the river rushes
by, the earth falling
into the running
water

Our bed of grass.
Trains rattle
east to stock yards.
Eyes of cattle between
box car slats painted barn-red

Soil on your cheek. You hold
my hand to the light,
our faces miniatures in the shine
of the other's eyes.

Poplars, birch-light,
the hard blue hovering over
us like mother love
or the shawl of cornflowers we tore
from the earth

High on the hill, people in chairs
on the porch, time streaming
through the house

Our tender mouths,
our tender arms,
How could
we know that beneath
us a god roams
with dirt
in his mouth

Jane Downs lives in Kensington, CA with her husband and dog. She received her BA in English from Syracuse University and her MA from Mills College. She is an editor and writer of poetry, fiction, and nonfiction. She left her position with the University of California Press in 2007 to cofound with book artist Marie Dern Red Berry Editions, an independent publishing house.

Her work received first place in both the 1997 Artists Embassy Contest and the 2003 Tide Pool Poetry Contest. One of her poems was published and was first runner-up in the winter 2002 Lullwater Literary Review. Her work has appeared in numerous publications including Ashville Poetry Review, FIELD, Folio, Green Hills Literary Lantern, The North American Review and Ninth Letter. She also served as coeditor of *Cloud View Poets, An Anthology: Master Classes With David St. John*, which was published in 2005. Her novel, *The Sleeping Wall*, was a finalist in the Chiasmus Press book contest. Her chapbook, *April Elegy*, received Special Merit recognition from the 2011 Jessie Bryce Niles Chapbook Contest sponsored by the Comstock Review and will be published by Kattywompus Press in 2012. She is the featured poet in the upcoming Psychological Perspectives, Volume 55, issue 4, 2012. She is currently working on her letterpress chapbook *Adirondack Dream*.

NAOMI RUTH LOWINSKY

"What became of our fierce flowering?"

Dear Sister-in-Poetry:

We have been sharing and critiquing each other's poems for forty years, and still your work sings, dances, leaps off the page. Your poetry introduces us to a rich world. Your source is the deep seas of the psyche, from which life and dream arise. The poems are as liquid as they are lyrical, as we navigate the rivers of a woman's experience. You have written your life since I have known you, but now the waters are rising, the deep seas overflow as the ice melts, and in Nebraska this summer thousands of fish are dying, as the rivers heat and run dry. In your poetry you bravely encounter what we are experiencing, and the river of Self, the river you ride as a dolphin-daughter of the Muse, still flows freely.

In *Because The Mountain Is My Companion* you gather the "leaders of nations," "Santa," and "the Great White Bear," and they all find room and render meaning in the spaciousness of your poem:

> On the news the leaders of nations gather
> to argue about carbon footprints
> while in the city dozens of red and white Santas
> mostly without umbrellas/-
> are gathering in United Nations Plaza

> Because the North Pole where Santa makes gifts
> is under water
> And the Great White Bear has walked to the end
> of his melting world
> Because all our lives there's been some catastrophe
> just behind us/
> just before us

But you never turn away. You don't hide. You turn to the mountain:

> Because the mountain knows the eons in its bones
> it is a patient, broad shouldered bearer
> of wind, sun, rain, change ...
> I ask it to teach me the long slow way ...

Your poems have always included the mythic and the archetypal, and you remember to remember 'the ancient ones.' But you also sing of your romance with nature, intermingling the species, the sun, the hills, giving them each other's characteristics, in *Where Coyote Bush Roams:*

> We were high on the sky when we lived on that
>   ridge high
> on the red tailed hawk high
> on the long green rumps of the hills going yellow
> while the sun did its dance from winter to summer
> and back high on our ridge after work while the fog
> flowed over

Didn't we once worry that writing about specific events would date our work? Now the human-made disasters we are continually experiencing become milestones in our life. They call to us as strongly as the archetypal and the eternal, for each jeopardizes and destroys the animal and plant life people of the Privileged

World are finally learning to value - not for food, or clothing, but for their own sake.

BP's oil spill in the Gulf of Mexico was one of those human-made disasters. In *Invoking Patiann Rogers During the Oil Spill* you address Patiann, the poet of species:

> If I had your Audubon eye-to describe how the
> least tern sits on her eggs, how the pelican makes
> her/ nest could we protect their hatchlings? Could
> we rescue
> the oil clogged sea turtle, the laughing gull
>   the meandering crab dodging balls of tar, with
> poems?

Your song has become a dirge, a psalm, a new sea chanty of imperiled waters.

Since it has been so long since the buffalo roamed, they have become spectral figures in our imagination, or we see a small herd captured in a fenced green, to prove they are still alive. Years ago I saw the great herds running across the Serengeti, and realized that once such multitudes crossed our plains as well. In *Where the Buffalo Roam*, a great herd appeared to you driving Highway 24, "It *was a* thundering ghost herd of *buffalo that* shouldered the moon *out* of her *sky*," you write, and suddenly we enter the 'Old World':

> The ghost dancers stamped and beat their drums
> They chanted the world before *Highway 24* when
> earth
> *was* home to the *buffalo*
> when the people followed the dance
> of the sun, when they knew each *story* of *rock*
> each spirit of mountain, of tree
> *what* flowered, *what* died, *what* came *back*

You know that people are searching for those stories, dear Sister-in-Poetry, they believe that indigenous knowledge will be key to our survival if our own disaster-prone civilization - dissolves? explodes? Who knows if that is the Path? But when rocks, and trees and mountains were considered animate they were our guidelines, our ancient Global Positioning System, their voice telling us to turn West or stay on this road. Now - in this moment - on Highway 24, do we know which direction to take?

Sisters of My Time is also a lament:

> .....Don't you remember....
> how that Old Black Magic revealed Herself to us
> —gave us the fever
> the crazy nerve to burn bras, leave husbands,
> grow animal hair under our arms?

And then the tone changes, as you summon us, not with the ram's horn, but in the voice of the Ewe, in the time of the Crone:

> It's our time, Sisters, to gather
> what spells we know, what seeds we've cultivated
> what Oracle speaks in our dreams, for the root cellars
> of memory, the mason jars of prayer—emergency rations—
> for the daughters of the daughters of our daughters

May all who read this respond to your call.

BECAUSE THE MOUNTAIN IS MY COMPANION

Because it meanders from coyote yellow
        to occasional green
Because we know that temperatures are rising—
        we never expected this sudden freeze—

Because the mountain reached into cold wet skies this morning
And gathered itself a celestial garment of snow
        as though it had ascended
        become an Alp
        a Himalaya

Because my tawny old Devil Mountain
        is a suddenly wild thing of snow and of ice
I try to put these things together—how green
        the hills glow along the freeway
On the news the leaders of nations gather
        to argue about carbon footprints

while in the city dozens of red and white Santas—
        mostly without umbrellas—
        are gathering in United Nations Plaza

Because the North Pole where Santa
        makes gifts
        is under water

And the Great White Bear has walked to the end
of his melting world

Because all our lives there's been some catastrophe
just behind us
just before us

You could hide under your desk—protect
the back of your neck...

or you could get in your car and drive back
to the mountain
which has descended
to its essential coyote yellow
its occasional splashes of green

Because the mountain knows the eons in its bones
it is a patient, broad shouldered bearer
of wind, sun, rain, change.........

I ask it to teach me the long slow way...

WHERE COYOTE BRUSH ROAMS

Well they'd made up their minds to be everywhere because why not.
W.S. Merwin

We were high on the sky when we lived on that ridge   high
on the red tailed hawk   high
on the long green rumps of the hills going yellow
while the sun did its dance from winter
to summer and back   high
on our ridge after work while the fog flowed over
the darkening hills we poured red wine on the earth   high
on escape from the city's exhaust   high
on the song of the frogs in the pond
some man had made

                    never mind

that the pines and the cottonwood trees
knew they didn't belong up there   never mind
that electrical towers asserted their rights
that coyote brush said the land was its own
that the ridge wanted fire and we did not
we weed whacked   cleared   cut down those pines   never mind
that we heard their cries in the night
though they never belonged up there   never mind
that the frogs went away one day and so did we...

The ancient ones who walked these lands
who made their arrows from coyote brush

knew not to make one's home on a ridge
for a ridge will insist on fire

      home is in a valley
      by a river among cottonwoods

We live in the valley now where once there was a river
             where frogs once sang in spring

                        never mind

INVOKING PATIANN ROGERS DURING THE OIL SPILL

> *I thank the distinct edges*
> *Of the sixspined spider crab for their peculiarities*
> *And praise the freshwater eel for its graces.*
> Patiann Rogers

If I knew as much science as you, Patiann
the migratory patterns, mating rituals, feeding behavior
of all those creatures engulfed in sludge
would be in this poem. Would that help
those whose feathers are encrusted in crude
those whose webbed feet can't swim
those with gaping mouths—dead on the beach?

If I had your Audubon eye—to describe how the least tern
sits on her eggs, how the pelican makes her nest—
could we protect their hatchlings? Could we rescue
the oil clogged sea turtle, the laughing gull
the meandering crab dodging balls of tar, with poems?

Me? I get visions, and their unbearable
music—there's a dragon fly with oil
weighted wings, there's a blackened egret...
This is a dirge for the blue fin tuna —
They've lost their spawning grounds
in an ocean gone mad with black blood

If we could create an amulet, Patiann
of feather and fin, of marsh grass and mystical measures
of dolphin song, could we bring back the deep sea roe

or are we washed up too
in the Gulf
between how we are all connected-pelicans, poets, blue fin tuna -
and what has become of our world?

WHERE THE BUFFALO ROAM

A sky herd of buffalo stampeded the moon—I saw it
driving on 24. The radio said

the shadow of earth would steal the moon—
our only moon—but I tell you

It was a thundering ghost herd of buffalo
that shouldered the moon out of her sky

The moon disappeared in her deerskin dress
The ghost dancers stamped and beat their drums

They chanted the world before Highway 24
when earth was home to the buffalo

when the people followed the dance
of the sun, when they knew each story of rock

each spirit of mountain, of tree
what flowered, what died, what came back

as the moon came back in her deerskin dress—
our only moon—

in her radiant light
I looked at the sky over 24

but the buffalo were gone…

SISTERS OF MY TIME

What became of our fierce flowering? Don't you remember
how that Old Black Magic revealed Herself to us—
gave us the fever
the crazy nerve to burn bras, leave husbands, grow animal hair?
We knew Her belly laugh, Her circle dance
Her multiple orgasms—It was Our Period.

What became of us—Our Period long gone—stuck
in traffic jams, eaten by Facebook—gone stale
amidst the unwept unsayable? Some of us burst
our vessels. Some of us descended into cellars—
ghosts among the apricot preserves.

Meanwhile our bones thin, our skin loosens, our hands
can't handle a mason jar. And our Red Queen, what of her?
Her rain forests are bleeding out. Her corn won't tassel,
Her cattle are dying of thirst, Her Ivory Billed Woodpecker—
that God Almighty Bird—has not been heard for a generation.

Our Lady of Ripening's gone on a rampage—hot flashes
in the heartland, fire in the forest, flood
in the bayou, weeping
ice caps. Our grandchildren starve
for Her belly laugh, Her circle dance.

Now is the time, Sisters, to gather
what spells we know, what seeds we've cultivated

what Oracle speaks in our dreams, for the root cellars
of memory, the mason jars of prayer—emergency rations—
for the daughters of the daughters of our daughters

long after that Old Black Magic

has spirited us away......

Naomi Ruth Lowinsky is a widely published poet and the author of several poetry collections including *Adagio & Lamentation*. She is the winner of the Obama Millennium Award for a poem about Obama's grandmother.

The Sister from Below: When the Muse Gets Her Way, tells stories of her pushy muse. She is also the co-editor, with Patricia Damery, of *Marked by Fire: Stories of the Jungian Way*.

Lowinsky teaches and lectures in many settings. She is an analyst member of the San Francisco Jung Institute and Poetry Editor of *Psychological Perspectives*.

It is an honor to be the publisher of *The Book of Now: Poetry for the Rising Tide*. To Anita Endrezze, Crystal Good, Dunya Mikhail, Frances Hatfield, Jane Downs, Leah Shelleda, and Naomi Ruth Lowinsky, I would like to express my sincere gratitude, for allowing Fisher King Press to publish poets of such venerated caliber. It is my hope that your mighty voices encompass the entire world and your messages reach and touch the hearts of humanity as a whole. It is my hope that your most worthy offerings are genuinely received and deeply understood.

Mel Mathews, Publisher
Fisher King Press

other il piccolo editions

After the Jug Was Broken
by Leah Shelleda, 1st Ed. Trade Paperback, 90 pp, 2010
— *ISBN 978-1-926715-46-9*

Sundered
by Phyllis Stowell 1st Ed. Trade Paperback, 81 pp, 2012
— *ISBN 978-1-926715-72-8*

Telling the Difference
by Paul Watsky, 1st Ed. Trade Paperback, 81 pp, 2010
— *ISBN 978-1-926715-00-1*

The Sister From Below: When the Muse Gets Her Way
by Naomi Ruth Lowinsky, 1st Ed., Trade Paperback, 248pp, 2009
— *ISBN 978-0-9810344-2-3*

Adagio & Lamentation
by Naomi Ruth Lowinsky, 1st Ed. Trade Paperback, 90 pp, 2010
— *ISBN 978-1-926715-05-6*

Phone Orders Welcomed
Credit Cards Accepted
In Canada & the U.S. call 1-800-228-9316
International call +1-831-238-7799
www.fisherkingpress.com

Made in the USA
Charleston, SC
21 November 2012